Life Coaching for
Latter Day Saints

Life Coaching for Latter Day Saints

Optimism

Motivation

Values

Goals

Alan Strong

British Library Cataloguing In Publication Data
A Record of this Publication is available
 from the British Library

ISBN 1846854245
978-1-84685-424-5

First Published 2006 by

Exposure Publishing, an imprint of Diggory Press,
Three Rivers, Minions, Liskeard, Cornwall, PL14 5LE, UK
WWW.DIGGORYPRESS.COM

Printed on Acid Free Paper

<u>Dedication</u>

This book is dedicated to my wife

And my family, they are my

Motivation and my Inspiration

Contents

About the author

Alan Strong

Alan Strong is a successful, licensed and certified, practising therapist in Neuro Linguistic Programming (NLP), Time Line Therapy™, Hypnotherapy, Psychotherapy and Counselling, being recognised and accredited both in the USA and UK.

He is a member of the Church of Jesus Christ of Latter Day Saints, a convert to the religion from sincere missionary work in 1989. Married to Michelle, his eternal companion, with six grown up children, and two grandchildren (to date). A member of the Shrewsbury ward (UK) and living in Shrewsbury, in the County of Shropshire, England.

Alan is in the process of undertaking seminars and workshops for businesses and within the church, as well as offering his services as a therapist to families, couples and individuals by appointment within his practise.

This is Alans first book to be published in this field, with a second book already well under way with an expected publication date in early 2007.

Email: a_charles_strong@hotmail.com

135 York House, Shoplatch, Shrewsbury, Shropshire, SY4 3HS, England

Chapter One

Life Coaching for Latter Day Saints – Starting out

Life Coaching for Latter Day Saints

Starting out

Before you start to read this book, I would like you to consider why you bought this book. At first, asking you to consider why you bought this specific book may not seem a serious question, but bear with me, why did you buy it?

As you ponder your answer to that question, let me suggest to you, things you may wish to consider. You may have decided that now is the time to change, a time for you, a time for right now. Maybe, just maybe, you want to make the most of you and what you can achieve. They are just a few possibilities, give it some time to think on this, and then, go right ahead and read this book, read it and work with it, right now.

A few more questions:

Are you ready to change? To move forward to the real you?

Do you want to change? To take charge of your future?

Do you want to set your life in a direction of your choosing?

Do you want to become a "cause" person instead of an "effect" person?

Let me explain about "cause and effect".

Various studies have found that an average of 98 people out of every 100 are essentially "effect" people. They allow their lives to be driven by the thoughts and actions of others, they don't act, they only react.

"Cause" people are those that make things happen, they are the people who initiate action and move forward with their lives, without the dictates of others. This doesn't mean that they don't interact and are not influenced by others, it just means that they will be the "cause" of what happens in their lives and take responsibility for what happens.

Another question to ask yourself:

Do you allow others to dictate or over influence your life and the direction you are going?

Now is the time to set your own direction, to understand what your own inner core values are, what your goals are, and how you are going to achieve them.

Don't read this book unless you are ready to change and you want to change, right now.

Make yourself comfortable, wherever you are at, just make yourself comfortable and relax, totally relax, that's right.

Relax yourself and clear your mind of all things around you.

As your mind clears

Relax

Think about who you are.

What you are

Where did you come from

And

Where are you going

Allow yourself to relax in to these thoughts

Relax in to your thoughts

Relax in to your mind.

Bring your thoughts to one's of happiness

To times of motivation and good feelings

And again

Let yourself relax.

Do you want to take control of your life?

Then use this book as your first step.

You will learn about you and your core values, what makes you, who you are, what is important to you, what will give you happiness in life, where do you want to go.

You will move on to how to set goals and most importantly, how to achieve them, you will allow yourself to grow, to progress with your life in a way that will keep a smile on your face and hope in your heart.

As you continue to read this book, take regular time out to enter in to prayer, so that Heavenly Father is included and is a part of this wonderful thing that you are undertaking, at this time.

Chapter Two

Trees

At this time, have you ever considered yourself as a tree, a tree that will allow Jesus Christ, the carpenter to mould you, to work with you, to mould you, the tree in to something great. Christ is the centre of our beliefs and our lives. Strive to attain a Christ like attitude in all things and strive to be that which you were intended to be.

I would like to tell you a story, a beautiful story that I hope and pray will inspire you to greatness.

Once upon a time (I do like stories that start like that), there was a hill covered in trees, and some of these trees were discussing one with another what their hopes and dreams were. Now three trees that would consider themselves friends were deep in to their discussion. The first tree said "I hope some day to be made in to a chest, a treasure chest. I could be filled with many precious things, gold, silver and gems, I could be decorated with the most beautiful of carvings and I would be something that all others admire".

The second tree said "Someday I want to be a ship, a mighty ship. I will be used to take great kings and queens across the seas and sail to the most important places in the world. Everyone will feel safe within me because of the strength of my timbers and how well I was made".

It was now the turn of the third tree, and he said "I don't want any woodsman to chop me down, I want to grow and grow, to be the tallest and straightest tree in the forest. People will be able to see me from great distances, on top of the hill, they will be able to look up at my branches and think of the heavens and God, and how close I am to reaching them. I will be the greatest tree of all time and people will always remember me.

After many years of growing and praying that their dreams will come true, a group of woodsmen approached the trees. One of the woodsmen came up to the first tree and said "This looks like a good quality tree, I think I should be able to sell the wood to a carpenter" ..... and he began to cut the tree down. The tree was very happy because he knew within his heart that the carpenter that was spoken of, would make him in to a treasure chest, just as he had always dreamed.

Another woodsman walked up to the second tree and said "This looks like a mighty, strong tree, I should be able to sell the wood to the artisans in the shipyard". The second tree was also very happy, because he knew that he was about to fulfil his dream and become a mighty ship.

As a woodsman approached the third tree, the tree began to shake and was frightened, because he knew that if they cut him down, his hopes and dreams would not come true. The woodsman said "I don't need anything special from my tree, so I will just take this one". And the third tree was cut down.

At the carpenters, the first tree was made in to a feed box for animals. He was then located in a small barn and filled with hay. This was nothing like what he had hoped and prayed for.

The artisans within the shipyard worked upon, the second tree, and he was cut up and made in to a small fishing boat. His hopes and dreams of becoming a mighty ship and carrying kings had come to an end.

The third tree was worked upon, he was cut and hewn in to large pieces and left alone in the dark of the large timber storehouse. As the years went by the trees forgot about their earlier hopes and dreams.

One day.......a man and a woman came to the barn. The woman gave birth to a child and they placed the baby in the hay in the feed box that had been made from the first tree. The man wished that he could have made a proper crib for the baby, but this manger would have to do. The first tree could feel the importance of this event and knew that it had held the greatest treasure of all time.

Many years later, a group of men, got in the fishing boat that had been made from the second tree. One of the men was tired and went to sleep. While they were out on the water, a great storm rose up and the tree started to question itself, as to whether it was strong enough to keep the men safe. The men awoke the sleeping man, who stood up and said "peace" and the storm stopped. It was then that the tree knew that it had carried the King of Kings in its small fishing boat.

The third tree was still in the dark of the timber storehouse, when one day someone came and got it. It was carried through streets filled with many people who mocked and spat upon the man who was carrying it. When they came to a stop, the man was nailed to the tree and raised in to the air to die atop a mighty hill. When Sunday came, the tree began to realise

20

that it was strong enough to stand at the top of the hill and be as close to God as was ever possible, because Jesus had been crucified upon it.

When things don't seem to be going your way, always know that God has a plan for you. If you place your trust in him, you will achieve. Each of the trees got what they wanted, just not in the way they had imagined. We don't always know what God's plans are for us. We just know that his ways are not our ways, but his ways are always the best.

Pray to have Heavenly Father with you as you set out on this journey of self discovery and adventure, as you undertake these early steps in life coaching and know he will be there to support you, whatever comes your way.

Chapter Three

The right frame of mind – Optimism

The right frame of mind – Optimism

During the time I have been studying psychology I have found it most intriguing that, a part of what makes us human, the area of the brain right behind the forehead, an area known as the frontal lobes - constantly thinks about the future, about creating, reviewing, rehearsing, and discarding various scenarios about what will and what will not happen, what may or may not happen. The possibilities are endless.

This projecting into the future is something everybody does, it is normal, healthy, human behaviour, or, so it should be.

If, as we are projecting our thoughts into the future, and we are utilising positive, healthy thoughts and feelings, then this projecting in to the future will remain healthy and positive, giving us something wonderful to aim for.

However, all too often, those projections are not based on positive, uplifting, optimistic thoughts. Instead, they consist of mainly negative thoughts, which pull us down.

We are not born pessimistic. When we come in to this world as a newly born bouncing little baby, it is acknowledged by most people, that we have genetic programming, of which, many believe only has a limiting influence on our behaviour, but little else. Therefore, on this basis, everything else that comes in to our heads, everything that we come to believe, our attitudes, our core values in life, will come directly and indirectly from the influences of others, they will come from what I like to refer to as, life programming.

As the years pass, and we progress through life, the things that happen or don't happen, the things that people say, what people do, how they act, how they treat us, and many, many more influencing factors tend to dictate the actions and thoughts we choose. As to whether we are going to be optimistic or pessimistic. I say that we choose, and some may find that hard to accept, but it's true. It's the way it happens, we choose to believe the input in to our brains that we receive from others. Sometimes, if our mood is not good, we will take something from someone else, something that was of positive intention, and change it to something negative and pessimistic. Many people will influence us with their comments, their opinions, often extracted out of context from their own perceived failures. We do not have to accept this.

The thoughts and comments of others are not facts, they are merely their opinions, their views of what has or may have happened. It doesn't have to be your view, it's your choice, think for yourself, act on your thoughts, be positive and make things happen in your life, for you, for good and for happiness.

We may be very fortunate and have an upbringing where the influences are mainly positive, this is great, use it to your benefit and help to influence others around you with your positive, optimistic thought patterns, share what you have and know is good for you. It's just like sharing the Gospel, it will make you and others around you happy, what more could you want?

Optimism is the fuel of heroes and achievers, the enemy of despair and despondency, the creator of the future and a fulfilling life.

Those of you, who think of yourselves as rational, clear-headed people, may say, "I'm neither an optimist nor a pessimist. I'm a realist." In making such a reasonable-sounding statement you would intend to express a commitment to truth, sound judgment, and rationality.

I would suggest that we could be both optimists and realists at the same time. The nature of the world means that to be realistic we must normally be optimistic.

Optimism and pessimism are more than attitudes toward truth. If I were to say that, I am an optimist, I am saying more than that I expect life to get better. That is a purely factual belief. It is either right or wrong. Optimists go beyond holding certain beliefs about the future. They also display certain attitudes. Optimism and pessimism involve not detached estimates of the objective probability of good and bad events in the future, but personal commitments to certain modes of thinking and behaving. By mastering these modes of thinking and adopting optimistic attitudes, we can profoundly influence our thinking, behaviour, happiness, and achievement.

A definition of optimism, which will focus us on the essentials, is:

An active, empowering, constructive attitude that creates conditions for success by focusing and acting on possibilities and opportunities.

Optimism, the opposite of pessimism, exemplifies a life view where a person looks upon the world as a positive place. Optimists generally believe that people and events are inherently good. They have a so-called "positive" outlook on life, believing that things will work out in the end. A common conundrum illustrates optimism versus pessimism with the question, does one regard a given glass of water as half full or as half empty? Conventional wisdom expects optimists to reply with half full and pessimists to respond with half empty.

Personal optimism correlates strongly with self-esteem, with mental and psychological well-being and with personal health.

From various studies, it has been established that a very high percentage of adults are pessimists. Not many (if any) people will admit to being a pessimist. They may admit to not being an optimist, but they won't admit to being a pessimist. You see, to admit such a thing is acknowledgement. Such acknowledgement is the first step to being able to change. Change is something you have to come out of your comfort zone for, and that's where it is hard.

If we are going to be optimists, we may have quite a fight on our hands, but it will be worth it, remember, from the positive point of view, for every 20 people you know or meet, at least one, and possibly two, will be optimists. And these are the people that will succeed in life. Being a pessimist now, doesn't mean you always will be. You can change, but it isn't easy. It takes work and commitment from you. All change is by you, within you and for you.

Let me repeat that for emphasis:

All change is by you, within you and for you.

As life and other people try to put rubbish in to our heads, thoughts that tell us that we can't succeed, that we will fail, that we are not good enough, that we are not worthy. Stand up for yourself. Refuse to accept those thoughts and words, be positive, be optimistic and allow yourself to live. Life makes us judgemental, but only if we choose to be, it's your choice. You can throw out the negative opinions of others, their perceptions of failure. Refuse to accept their limitations, and instead, look to yourself, believe in yourself, and grow.

Grow to the very heights that you are capable of. And you will not know how high that is, until you get there.

A saying I once heard is: "people who constantly keep their feet on the ground, will struggle to fly". Think about it.

Take that chance, you may enjoy it, you have nothing to lose, except that which you don't really want. Take that first step out of your comfort zone, with a happy positive frame of mind, start to grow, and be that which you were meant to be, it's your choice.

There have been many studies on optimism, and they have all established much the same findings

1.   Optimists live a longer life than pessimists. (Although the life of a pessimist will probably feel longer).

2.   Optimists suffer from fewer and less severe diseases.

3.   Optimists are much healthier than pessimists.

4.   Optimists are just happier.

Besides these obvious health benefits, optimism also brings about a higher quality of life. Applying optimism within the various aspects of our lives, the spiritual, mental and physical, will greatly enhance our enjoyment and therefore quality of life.

We are told within the scriptures that we are here not only to learn, but also to have joy, to have happiness. To live as a pessimist, you cannot achieve these things, you cannot enjoy the blessings of life to the level Heavenly Father intended. You restrict anything and everything as to how far you can go, you will keep your feet on the ground, and not fly. Acknowledge, accept and then change, it's your choice.

Be positive and know there are no limitations. It is important to change negative thought patterns in to positive ones. Optimism will come automatically from positive thought patterns.

Look to your quality of life. Manifested as greater success, greater happiness and greater love. A life of accomplishment. A life to be lived, full and rich. A life worth living. A life you can be rightfully proud of. A life you can truly enjoy, no matter what comes your way.

Optimists are more successful than pessimists, optimistic politicians win more elections, optimistic students get higher grades, optimistic athletes win more contests and optimistic sales people make more money. Why is this so? Because optimism and pessimism are both self-fulfilling prophecies. If you think a set back is permanent, why would you change it? Pessimistic explanations tend to make you feel defeated, making you less likely to take constructive action. Optimistic explanations, on the other hand, make you more likely to act. If you think a set back is only temporary, you are more likely to do something about it.

This book highlights just a few of the benefits of being optimistic in your outlook, and being an optimist in your approach. Remember, they are for your benefit, your well-being, your growth and your quality of life. It really is your choice.

Improving your optimism could be one of the most important and fulfilling actions you can take to improve your life. It will not and does not come automatically, though. It takes effort, a lot of effort. It takes deliberate, conscious awareness of your thoughts and feelings. And then acting on that awareness.

You may wish to note, that mood also has an influence on whether optimistic or pessimistic thoughts dominate your brain. Working to gain control over moods can result in more positive thinking. In turn, positive thinking will result in better moods.

Optimists tend to use exercise, yoga and even "putting on a happy face" as ways to relax and thereby improve their moods.

There are many ways that will work for you as an individual, to help you lift yourself when your mood isn't that great. Take the time to find what those ways are, practice them and make them a part of your life.

Some of the people reading this book, who know me personally, will know that I have a favourite song that I sing. A song that lifts my mood, a song that lifts my very soul, and usually lifts the mood of those around me.

I understand from others that there are far more verses to my song, than I have actually ever learnt, but my little part, what I call my song, is enough for me and it goes like this:

So let the sunshine in,

take it with a grin,

smilers never lose,

frowners never win,

so let the sunshine in,

take it with a grin,

smilers never lose,

so let the sunshine in.

It's all down to you, it's your choice!

Chapter Four
Motivation

Motivation

Ask any person who is successful in whatever he or she is doing what motivates him/her, and very likely the answer will be "goals". Goal Setting is extremely important to motivation and success.

So what motivates you?

Why are you doing what you do now? If you are in a certain job because that's what your parents or your wife/husband want, you may find it difficult to motivate yourself. Sure, it's possible to succeed with someone else providing the motivation for you. ("If you graduate from college, I'll give you a car!" or worse "If you don't graduate from college, you won't get a car.") But motivation that comes from within really makes the difference.

Certainly, you need some intelligence, knowledge base, study skills, time management skills, and many other skills throughout life, but if you don't have motivation, you won't get far.

Think about this analogy. Consider that you have a car with a full tank of gas, a well-tuned engine, good set of tires, quadraphonic CD system, and a sleek, polished exterior. There it sits on the drive. This car has incredible potential. (Have you heard that before?) However, until a driver sits behind the wheel, puts the key in the ignition, and starts it up, the car doesn't function. It can't fulfil its potential until you get it started. The Key is Motivation.

Interest is an important motivator for anything you undertake. So is an acknowledgement that you don't know everything and therefore have a desire to learn. When you link interest and desire together, you create success. Often success in an endeavour leads to more interest and a greater desire to learn, creating an upward spiral of motivation toward a goal you have established.

So be honest with yourself. Are you genuinely interested in doing what you do, being what you are, going wherever it is that you're heading? Have you set realistic goals for yourself? How can you develop the internal motivation that really counts? When it comes to motivation, knowing is not as important as doing.

Motivation starts with the desire to be free, to be free from dependency on others, freedom to live the lifestyle we dream of, freedom to explore our ideas. Total freedom is not possible or desirable, but the struggle to achieve that ideal is the basis for motivation.

Motivation is built.

Motivation starts with a need, vision, dream or desire to achieve the seemingly impossible. Creativity is associated with ideas, projects, and goals, which can be considered a path to freedom.

Developing and maintaining a love of learning lifestyle, becoming involved with risky ventures, and continually seeking new opportunities to learn what works and does not work, all this will help.

Develop and maintain a desire to overcome barriers and to bounce back from discouragement or lack of success. Learn to tolerate the agony that lack of success brings. In any endeavour, that is worthwhile, barriers and lack of success will be there. Bouncing back requires creative thinking, as it is a learning process. In addition, bouncing back requires starting again at the beginning.

How to Succeed at Motivation

a. Set a major goal, but follow a path. The path has many smaller goals that go in many directions. When you learn to succeed at smaller goals, you will be motivated to set and achieve greater goals. But don't let that stop you from setting greater goals right now, if you're ready for it, then go for it.

b. Develop the habit of finishing projects and achieving your goals. Learn to finish what you start. A part-finished project is of no use to anyone, but especially not you. Giving up is a habit, a bad habit that needs to be changed.

c. Socialise with others of similar interest. Mutual support is motivating. You will be influenced enough to develop the attitudes of your best friends. If they are losers, complainers, pessimists, then you are likely to be all those things. If the people you socialise with are optimistic, happy winners, you are more likely to be an optimistic, happy winner. To be an achiever you need to associate with achievers.

d.   Learn how to learn. Dependency on others for knowledge supports the habit of procrastination. You have the ability to learn without instructors. In fact, when you learn the art of self-education you will find, and possibly create, opportunity to find success beyond your wildest dreams.

e.   Harmonize your talents and skills with interest that motivates. Your talents and skills create motivation, motivation creates persistence and persistence gets the job done.

f.   Increase knowledge of subjects that inspire you. The more you know about a subject, the more you will want to learn about it. A self-propelled upward spiral develops. Try applying this to your scripture reading, watch what happens.

g.   Not succeeding and being able to bounce back are elements of motivation. So take risks. Not succeeding is a learning tool. No one has ever succeeded at anything worthwhile without the things that went wrong, the struggles, the trials and tribulations. Use them as part of your motivation.

Analyse Your Comfort Zone

The Comfort Zone is your living environment, your school or working environment, and your church and social environments that you have grown used to. Your comfort zone influences the type of friends you make or people you associate with. Your comfort zone influences your life style.

Young people can adapt very easily, they can often adjust to changing comfort zones with ease. As we grow older and mature, the ability to adapt to wide-ranging comfort zones, for some reason becomes more difficult. This is again where the influences of others will programme us. Such programming is limiting and restrictive. Social prejudice narrows the comfort zone range. Read the following and see where your present comfort zone is.

1. I want to maintain my current comfort zone.

2. I am dissatisfied with my current conditions and want to move to a different comfort zone.

3. I have been suddenly moved out of my comfort zone and want to get back to my comfort zone as soon as possible.

4. I only make decisions when I have facts. My comfort zone is what I use as a decision making tool.

If you were content with your current comfort zone, then it is unlikely that you would be reading this book. Because you are reading, it is safe to assume that you want to make some changes in the way you live and work. Therefore, if you are dissatisfied with your current life style, you can make changes to it, by changing your comfort zone.

Comfort zones are directly related to your dreams or goals. In order to grow and change, you must first be discontent with your current comfort zone.

To change to a different life style, establish a new business, or succeed at something you haven't tried before. Understand that, all meaningful and lasting changes occur first in dreaming about what you want and then you work with it into reality. If you clearly imagine yourself as being and having the things you truly want, you will create a new picture of yourself. The old comfort zone, in time, will be unacceptable to you and you will find ways to acquire the new comfort zone.

The key to upgrading your comfort zone is to raise your self-image and level of what you expect or want first, and then you will find opportunity to make the goal reality.

The more clearly and vividly you dream your dream, repeated frequently, the stronger and more real the pictures on the unconscious level will become. Once your unconscious will accept the images and expectations, the unconscious will go to work, searching for a way to bring it into reality. If you feel that these things are too good for you, you will find ways to fail.

You will find ways to acquire your dreams and, when ready, it will arrive faster than you ever thought possible. In effect, what you are doing is deliberately preparing yourself for self-fulfilling prophecy.

As has been written in many books and said many times:

Whatever the mind can conceive and believe, it can achieve.

Negative comfort zones can be overcome by setting and thinking about positive goals. What you think about and what you expect, be it positive or negative, this is your comfort zone.

**Chapter Five
Life Coaching**

Life Coaching

Life Coaching is something positive, exciting, enlightening, something to put a smile upon your face and then keep it there. Life coaching will help you to bring about so many things that you seek in life, to achieve your goals and help your families to achieve theirs as well. Life coaching is an ever developing, ever changing, increasingly popular method for helping people to help themselves, to fulfil the potential they have within themselves, to develop old skills, to learn and develop new skills, to find personal success in both a temporal and a spiritual sphere, to set and achieve goals, manage life change and deal with personal challenges.

As latter day saints we face many challenges within our lives here on earth. These challenges can, and often do, come from many different directions, sometimes expected, sometimes not. We strive to live by the standards and principles that have been set before us, not only by the teachings of Christ but also modern day revelation from our living prophet.

Life coaching can be effective in all situations and with all people, whether in the physical, mental or spiritual aspects of personal life, family life, church or business life. Within this book, you are given some of the ways in which you can bring about changes within your life, but essentially, it is you that will bring about those changes. This is the time to be excited by all those wonderful things that you can achieve. This book may be considered a toolbox of ideas, methodology and even more ideas. You are the artisan who will wield those tools and bring about the changes you seek, within you and about you.

Life coaching should not be viewed as training, in fact it is completely different to training, in that coaching draws out that which is within, rather than putting in, that which is without. Life coaching develops and empowers the person rather than imposing controls or restrictions on the person. Life coaching reflects rather than directs. Life coaching is an active, flexible, ever adapting, ever changing and enabling system of a non-prescriptive or instructional aspect.

Life coaching is non-judgemental, helping people to develop within themselves and to grow in as many areas as they will allow themselves to do so, nothing is impossible if you have faith and believe in yourself, believing that you are capable. Life coaching will help in establishing that belief within you, as a part of you, to stay with you, no matter what comes your way.

There is at this time a development of many separate coaching specialists, newly identified coaching disciplines in their own right, covering and filling an ever growing number of niche markets for life coaching skills.

Some of these specialists are: personal coaching and life coaching, coaching for life-change, parenting; self-fulfilment and self-discovery; career coaching for advancement and job choices; leadership and management coaching; coaching for sales and business success; executive coaching for corporate performance and director development.

There are many, many other aspects where there can be found specialist life coaches to assist in your personal development. Although there are all these various niche markets, the main core of life coaching is the same for all of them.

It is the intention of this book to put before you those skills that form the main core of life coaching, so that you can utilise them in whatever aspect of your life or the lives of your families as you feel fit. You decide what you can do, when you can do it and how you can do it.

Life coaching is a fast growing business skill, a recognised profession, one that is seeing rapid growth throughout it's many aspects, primarily because it helps people of all walks of life to rise to their fullest potential in all three of the fields of Mental, Physical and Spiritual well being.

Life coaching changes the approach that many people have to life. Approaches, which are often restrictive and debilitating. Allow yourself this opportunity to change you life for the better.

Do not continue with the reading of this book unless you are ready to change, ready to take control of your life, to take those first steps in the direction of fulfilling your ambitions in life.

Life coaching is about getting the very best out of someone and enabling him or her to make decisions that will improve their life. Life coaches can be hired for very many different and diverse reasons, for example: to climb the career ladder faster; to feel more fulfilled at work; to improve relationships with family and partners; to learn parenting skills that benefit both the child and parent; to gain a spiritual meaning to life, or a desire to 'get sorted'.

As a latter day saint, we are taught many things, not least of which are, to learn, to develop our talents, to fulfil our potential, physically, mentally and spiritually, and ultimately as we do all these things and more, to return to our heavenly father, knowing we have done the best we could in this life.

The Life coaching profession is growing and coaching is becoming widely acknowledged by people throughout the world. People have begun to realise that coaching can be highly effective and enabling in all aspects of their lives.

Coaching is a relatively new and somewhat different profession, it is not psychology, counselling or psychotherapy, although not excluded from those fields in effectiveness, in addition to having many overlaps of the skills and understandings utilised within its usage.

It is the intention of this book, not only to enable the reader to empower themselves to achieve their utmost potential with Life coaching skills, but also to include relevant and effective systems and ideas from Neuro Linguistic Programming, Hypnotherapy and Psychotherapy, as and when beneficial to you.

As you read through this book and put in to action the positive and motivating changes in your life, with the utmost in optimism, as you set your goals and bring about those achievements you seek, remember, this is about you now, as you are, and the future, as you can be. It is not about the past, it is not about those times you feel you failed, we are going forward, forward to success.

Remember that when things happened in the past, at that time it was the present, when things happen in the future, that will be the present, so with this in mind, nothing happens yesterday and nothing happens tomorrow, the only time anything happens is today, in the present, now, at this time. So make it happen, Now!

Chapter Six
Butt prints in the sand

Butt prints in the sand

One night I had a wondrous dream,

One set of footprints there was seen,

The footprints of my precious Lord,

But mine were not along the shore.

But then some stranger prints appeared,

And I asked the Lord "What have we here?"

Those prints are large and round and neat,

"But Lord, they are too big for feet."

"My child," He said in sombre tones,

"For miles I carried you alone.

I challenged you to walk in faith,

but you refused and made me wait.

You disobeyed,

you would not grow,

The walk of faith,

you would not show,

so I got tired,

I got fed up,

and there I dropped you on your butt."

"Because in life there comes a time,

When one must fight,

and one must climb,

When one must rise and take a stand,

Or leave their butt prints in the sand."

Chapter Seven
Establish your core values – who is the real you?

Establish your Core Values - Who is the 'real' you?

Modern life seems to demand that we are different people in different situations, but deep down we all hold core values that are the key to our true selves. Living in accordance with these is the secret to an authentic and fulfilling life.

Values are like our fingerprints, or like our DNA, no one's fingerprints or DNA are exactly the same, and you leave them all over everything you come in to contact with.

Everyone has a unique set of totally personal inner values and, even if you're not sure what they are, they will define and shape every aspect of your life. They are you.

Values are linked to our personal identity, so losing sight of your values is really losing sight of who you really are.

Living an authentic life is impossible until you have pinned your values down and acknowledged them. Until you have a solid foundation of personal values, then there is no point in creating any goals. It is to this end that we first establish your values, before helping you to create your goals.

Drawing out your inner personal values can sometimes be tricky. On the whole, it is much easier to define your life in terms of what you do, rather than asking what really motivates you to do it. What is central to your well-being? Integrity? Love? Honesty? Excitement?

If I were to ask you directly what is most important to you and what your values are, it just doesn't work. It is your unconscious mind that holds and activates your core values, and most people are not even aware of there existence. Thereby many people would not be able to answer the question, as they don't know what their inner personal values really are.

Isolating Values

Think about moments in your life when life has really felt good, times that have made you feel happiest. Remember what it was that made you feel most elated? It may be that getting your first job you feel independent, releasing you to create your own destiny. It could have been when you got married, when your children were born, when you graduated, there are so many possibilities. Look to see which themes repeat themselves throughout your other key memories – where they do, they are some of your more important core values.

Write here about your feel good moment number one

What was it?

When was it?

How did you feel?

What core values do you recognise?

Write here about your feel good moment number two

What was it?

When was it?

How did you feel?

What core values do you recognise?

Write here about your feel good moment number three

What was it?

When was it?

How did you feel?

What core values do you recognise?

Did you notice, that as you relived those feel good moments, as you thought about them, and as you wrote about them, they made you feel good once again.

It is worth remembering this and establishing ways of bringing those feel good moments to your conscious mind whenever you feel in need of them. They will help you to overcome times when you don't feel motivated, when you feel down and just plain grumpy.

Now I would like you to think of moments that did the opposite – times when you felt grumpy and sad, times when the world didn't seem to be that great a place to be in. Establish why did these moments make you feel like that? Question yourself honestly to get answers to these questions. Your answers will most likely be directly opposing your true values. For example, if a dominant parent bullied you, you may have felt restricted, so from this your core value could be freedom.

Write here about your feel bad moment number one

What was it?

When was it?

How did you feel?

What core values do you recognise?

Write here about your feel bad moment number two

What was it?

When was it?

How did you feel?

What core values do you recognise?

Write here about your feel bad moment number three

What was it?

When was it?

How did you feel?

What core values do you recognise'?

Again you will notice that as you relive those feel bad moments, they bring back all the old emotions and anger. We will not dwell on these too much or for too long, as our intention is to motivate and get you feeling good, and not the opposite.

So let's get back to those feel good moments. Take a little time to go back to what you previously wrote, look over what is there, see if you can add a little more and relive those moments in your mind again.

Having carried out the task of writing down your feel good and feel bad moments, and I hope you are feeling good about yourself at this moment in time. We are now going to look at people, not just any people, but people that you have come across in your life that you admire. Again you have to be honest with yourself here, and I am assuming that you have been all the way through the book so far, it is the only way that this will work, right now.

Consider the people carefully, not just the celebrities that you see from afar, the great sportsmen and women, the film stars, but consider those people that are around you, closest to you, people who have qualities that you truly admire. It may be your parents, grandparents, children, boss, colleague, neighbour, Bishop. In fact it could be anyone at all, just so long as there is something about him or her that you admire.

Before you start this exercise, here is a quiz, you don't actually have to do the quiz, just read it through from start to finish, and you will get the point, a pretty powerful one.

1. Name the 5 wealthiest people in the world.
2. Name five Olympic gold medal winners.
3. Name the last 5 winners of the Miss World contest.
4. Name 5 people who have won the Nobel prize.
5. Name 10 Oscar winners and the films they got them from.
6. Name the 5 top scorers in your favourite sport.

The point is that none of us remember the people who hit the headlines of yesterday. These people we asked you to name, they are not second rate achievers, they are the best in their fields. But the applause dies, Awards get dusty and achievements are forgotten. The accolades and certificates are buried with their owners.

Now consider this quiz. See how you do on this one.

1. Name 3 teachers who have aided your journey through school.
2. Name 3 friends who have helped you through a difficult time.
3. Name 5 people who have taught you something worthwhile.
4. Name 3 people at church who have inspired you.
5. Name 5 people who have made you feel appreciated.
6. Name 5 people who you enjoy spending time with.
7. Name 5 people who are unsung heroes.

The people who make a difference in your life are not the ones who have the most credentials, the most money, or have won the most awards. They are the ones who care. They are the ones who make a difference.

Set yourself on the path of being one of those great people who make a difference.

Now make a list of up to 10 people you most admire.

1.

2.

3.

4.

5.

6.

7.

8.

9.

10.

Now we will take this a little further.

Having established the ten people who you admire. The next ten pages have been set out for you to record, not only their names and who they are to you. But also to list the traits you most admire within them, and, where possible, with as much detail as you are able, give examples of when they have displayed these traits.

As you progress through the pages, you will probably discover that the traits you admire most, will repeat themselves within the different people you have chosen to write about, these will indicate more of your core values.

First person you most admire

Their name:

Their relationship to you:

The traits you admire and examples:

Second person you most admire

Their name:

Their relationship to you:

The traits you admire and examples:

Third person you most admire

Their name:

Their relationship to you:

The traits you admire and examples:

Fourth person you most admire

Their name:

Their relationship to you:

The traits you admire and examples:

Fifth person you most admire

Their name:

Their relationship to you:

The traits you admire and examples:

Sixth person you most admire

Their name:

Their relationship to you:

The traits you admire and examples:

Seventh person you most admire

Their name:

Their relationship to you:

The traits you admire and examples:

Eighth person you most admire

Their name:

Their relationship to you:

The traits you admire and examples:

Ninth person you most admire

Their name:

Their relationship to you:

The traits you admire and examples:

Tenth person you most admire

Their name:

Their relationship to you:

The traits you admire and examples:

Naming Core Values

From the list below, select ten of them that you feel are most important to you, values that you like and want to live by, put a circle around them to remind yourself, as you will want to refer to them again in a little while.

Love	Marriage	Respect
Security	Power	Achievements
Health	Passion	Acceptance
Happiness	Integrity	Humour
Children/Family	Success	Kindness
Adventure	Freedom	Independence
Travel	Trust	Excitement
Honesty	Compassion	Intimacy

Now you have identified some of your core values. The next step is to prioritise them.

Think long and hard about each of the core values you have identified; spend a few minutes interpreting each of your chosen values and what they mean to you.

An example of this is, if you list security, what would it take to make you feel secure? Money? Love? A pension plan?

You need to be sure that the goals you are pursuing will bring the results you need.

For example, if achievements and success are core values, what makes you feel a sense of achievement? If it's your family, then don't fool yourself that you will happily work at growing a business and working all the hours there are, while neglecting your family.

If success is a value, what kind of success, and in what? Business, Family, Church, the options are endless. But be certain that you are being true to yourself and looking at the real you, not the you that you might perceive that others want.

Taking those Core values you circled previously, I would like you to consider which are more important to you than others. Remember, there are no right or wrong answers to this exercise. There are no good or bad core values. It is what is important to you that we are trying to establish here. This is a priority list of what you, and only you find important as core values.

Write your prioritised list here, with the most important value at number one and then on to number ten:

1.

2.

3.

4.

5.

6.

7.

8.

9.

10.

As with all things positive, we also have to look at the negative. In order to fight your fears, and we all have them, you first of all have to be aware of what your negative emotions are, what is it that triggers your fears and then brings about negative reactions from you. Acknowledge to yourself that they really do exist and let us choose this as the time to confront them.

From the list below, choose two of the negative emotions shown, that you personally, would most like to avoid in your life.

Rejection	Anger	Frustration
Loneliness	Depression	Failure
Humiliation	Guilt	Abandonment

Write your two negative emotions here

The answers you have written in the previous box are those negative emotions that at this time in your life, will determine your behaviour in almost any environment, as well as define your positive core values.

If success were one of your core values, then you would set goals to achieve success, but you will only achieve success if you confront your fears of, say, for example, failure, if you don't confront your fears then your energies that you could have directed to achieving your goals will always be directed to avoidance (denying yourself) rather than fulfilment (being true to yourself).

You can only fulfil your core values by taking emotional risks, which means confronting those feelings you'd rather avoid.

I will repeat that, because it is one of those things that we would much prefer not to acknowledge.

You can only fulfil your core values by taking emotional risks, which means confronting those feelings you'd rather avoid.

Once you are aware of your key values then, it is much easier to stay true to your essential self and start mapping out goals.

Every person around you has a unique set of inner values, unique and different to those inside you. With this in mind it is easier to see that there are no right or wrong core values. Your values could be considered as your own personal toolbox. It is up to you how you will use those tools, for good or bad. There are therefore no good or bad values, only good or bad behaviour as to how you utilise those values.

There is no right or wrong in establishing core values. You are, who you are and your values, are what you need to live to in order to achieve success, and a feeling of well being within your life.

You will now have a much better idea as to what your core values are, they will define and shape every aspect of your life, so get to know them well, they are a part of who you are.

Remind yourself of the core values you established from those people who you admire. Look back at what you wrote about those people, think about what core values you admire. Are these the same as the core values you have? Once you are aware of your key values, it is much easier to stay true to your essential self and start mapping out goals.

What if you don't like the 'You' you Discover

It can often come as a shock to discover a set of core values that indicate you are not what you always believed or tried to fool yourself, you were. You may be more selfish, or materialistic than you believed, but don't worry, it isn't the end of the world.

There are no bad values. Only good or bad ways of expressing those values to others or yourself. It is not bad to be selfish if you respect other people and don't intentionally hurt them. Wanting to be rich is fine, but try to define it further. Is it just the money you want? Or is it security? Or even a sense of power?

Take each value and think about how it shapes the way you act. If you have learnt that you have a core value that you don't feel comfortable with, stand back for a few moments and think of different ways you could adapt your behaviour, which would make it more acceptable to you. Always focus on specific examples. If you discover you're not very tactile, work on improving your hugging skills.

Eventually, as you acknowledge and work with your values, you will find that you come round in a full circle. Values will alter over time as we get older, wiser and our lives change. Thinking about your behaviour and making an effort to adapt it, will lead you to new values and experiences, things that you would not want to miss out on. Remember, we are only on this earth the one time, so make the most of it.

Chapter Eight
What would you like to hear?

What would you like to hear?

I would like you to consider what other people think of you. And then, taking it a step further, what you would like others to think of you?

A Speech at your Funeral

I would like you to write a speech, not a long speech, just enough to fill the next two and a half pages (that's all the space I have left you, so you are somewhat limited to that). With this speech I would like you to imagine that you have died and that your funeral is taking place. Friends of yours are at the funeral and one of them is going to give a speech about you. What would you like to hear about yourself from your friend? This is one of the best ways I know of getting someone, namely you, to start thinking about your core values and the affect they can have on others as well as yourself. While doing this, look back over the core values you have already identified and the negative emotions as well, take your time and make the speech a good one.

Write the speech here, what would you like to hear about yourself?

Continue your speech here

Continue your speech here

Stay true to your essential self.

Chapter Nine
The Chart of Life

The Chart of Life

Are you happy with your life balance?

The ten sections shown in the chart of life, below and continued on the next page, represent a useful guide to the balance of our lives.

The chart is identified within each section as 0 out of 10 on the left, and the right edge as 10 out of 10. With the midway point of 5 out of 10 as being averagely okay, rank your level of satisfaction with each life area by putting a circle around the number that most represents where you feel you are at this time.

What you are aiming for is the left area of the chart to be larger than the right area – where it is much smaller, this is a sign that key values are not being honoured.

The Chart of Life

Work/career										
0	1	2	3	4	5	6	7	8	9	10

Physical environment										
0	1	2	3	4	5	6	7	8	9	10

Fun and recreation										
0	1	2	3	4	5	6	7	8	9	10

Personal growth										
0	1	2	3	4	5	6	7	8	9	10

Money										
0	1	2	3	4	5	6	7	8	9	10

Health										
0	1	2	3	4	5	6	7	8	9	10

Husband/wife/girlfriend/boyfriend										
0	1	2	3	4	5	6	7	8	9	10

Family										
0	1	2	3	4	5	6	7	8	9	10

Friends										
0	1	2	3	4	5	6	7	8	9	10

Church/spiritual										
0	1	2	3	4	5	6	7	8	9	10

Spend some time to consider what your chart of life shows.

Now I would like you to write some notes on what your chart of life shows to you.

Over the next 10 pages, I would like you to write notes on;

where you are now,

what is restricting you from growing in this particular area,

what skills or talents you need to obtain to overcome problems in this particular area,

and

what you would like to do to rectify in those areas where your key values are not being honoured.

work/career

physical environment

Fun and recreation

Personal growth

Money

Health

Husband/Wife/Girlfriend/Boyfriend

Family

Friends

Church/Spiritual

Chapter Ten
Setting and achieving your Goals

Setting your Goals

Before you set your individual goals, I would ask you to pray and meditate. Ask Heavenly Father to help you to know where you are weak, and where you are strong. What you need to improve, and what your goals in this life, really are.

Your patriarchal blessing will help you to understand what your individual goals could be.

Instruction and direction from Church leaders could help you in setting your individual goals.

Develop an attitude, make up your mind to be a greater man or woman than you have ever been before.

Listen to the instructions and suggestions that come from our Church leaders.

Most of all, consult your scriptures, pray, and then listen to the Lord.

Think of the things that you have read within this book, and so far as they approach your life in any way, see if you can use them to take you forward toward the perfection, which the Lord has asked of all of us.

On the path to achieving your goals, you may sometimes become discouraged. Perhaps you have felt so burdened with personal problems, pressures, and frustrations that you feel inadequate to deal with them.

Do you strongly doubt whether you have the ability to handle the things before you, things that the Lord had already blessed you with. Do you despair at the gap between the ideal and your own performance? Do you feel that you would never qualify for exaltation, never become perfect?

Then kneel with a contrite heart to get help from the Lord. Get help to set your goals.

The Lord does not give any commandment unless he prepares a way for us to accomplish it. And you can accomplish anything you put your mind to. Anything!

Read the scriptures and pray many times each day. Be determined to prepare yourself, ask the Lord for as much help as is needed. Do it now, and feel the difference in your life. Love it! Feel happier and more confident.

Achieving your goals will be easier if you eliminate from your life those things that discourage or stop you. Poor habits, undesirable companions, and negative thoughts in the form of anxieties, doubts, and fears will keep you from accomplishing righteous desires and ambitions.

Having a positive attitude will help you achieve the goals you will set for yourself. As you work daily for improvement, freely and fully enjoy each accomplishment, however small it may be. Begin to perfect yourselves. A certain degree of perfection is attainable in this life. Be confidant that one of the great desires of the Lord our God is that we shall keep that great commandment which says, 'Be ye therefore perfect.'.

Time to Set Your Goals

You should by now have discovered what some, if not all of your core values are.

Take the time to go back and remind yourself of your core values and negative emotions, do this as many times as you need to during completion of the next stage.

Each core value and each negative emotion affects how you think and shapes the way you act. You will have learnt a lot about you and what you stand for

We have looked at what you would like to hear as a speech at your own funeral. These things are very, very important to you and to the way you feel.

Time to consider what your goals in life are. Consider what you have learnt about yourself so far, as to core values and negative emotions. Consider what you included in your "funeral speech".

Realising what we want in life is the hardest part of goal setting, how do you know what you really want? The wheel of life that we completed earlier in the book, will have helped on your understanding for life goals.

When setting your goals, make them:

Positive

Within your control

Smart

Manageable

Varied

Measurable

Achievable

Realistic

Time bounded

The next eleven pages are there for you to set your goals in different areas of your life. Continue to refer to any previous part of this book to assist you in writing these goals. Do it all with a positive attitude. Do it prayerfully, and most of all, do it because you want to.

Life Goals:

- First Goal – work/career

- Second Goal - physical environment

- **Third Goal – fun and recreation**

- Fourth Goal – personal growth

- **Fifth Goal – Money**

- **Sixth Goal - Health**

- **Seventh Goal – Husband/Wife/Girlfriend/Boyfriend**

- **Eighth Goal - Family**

- **Ninth Goal – Friends**

- Tenth Goal – Church/Spiritual

- **Eleventh Goal – It's Your Choice!**

Achieving your Goals

You have established what your core values are.

You have established what your negative emotions are.

You have set a number of Life Goals within different aspects of your life, now is the time to set about achieving them.

Life is a journey into an unknown future. Our goals act as a compass, guiding us to better relationships, improved health and wealth, more job satisfaction and greater personal fulfilment. It is the goals we set that define the path to making our dreams come true.

Write them down. Read them and repeat them to yourself every day

Pray about them

Visualise achieving your goals, frequently

Action is vital, avoid procrastination and take small steps every day

If you feel stuck, ask yourself "what is the easiest step I can take now in the direction of what I want

Keep goals secret, they are a path to your dreams and are vulnerable to sabotage. The opinions of others can often water down that which we want to achieve.

As you learn and discover more, adjust your goals accordingly, replace goals that no longer inspire you

Learn from conflicting goals. It is in the trade-offs between wanting, for example, both more time and more money that we discover our true goals. It is the tough choices that define our lives

True goals are inspiring and exciting. If you lose your motivation, take a week out and then review. If your goal is not inspiring then abandon it, if it is important then you will return to it, trust your intuition, trust that which is inside you.

Enjoy the journey, not just the destination.

You are now on your way to achieving your goals.

The next book in this series, will deal with; Mind, Language and Communication, introducing you to Neuro Linguistic Programming (NLP), to explain how you can improve your communication with others.

Seek understanding of your wife or husband, your children, your parents, your boss, your colleagues, your subordinates, all those people at church. Learn what language they learn in. How do they think. How do they understand. Who is speaking the truth. What makes people respond positively and what makes them respond negatively. What makes them tick, truly understand them.

When you communicate, it has been established that; only 7% of the communication between two people, is the actual words they speak, 38% is the way they say them, and 55% is their body language, the simple communication within the unconscious mind. It doesn't matter how good the words are, if you don't get the rest right, the best they will understand is 7% of what you wanted to communicate.

Thank you for purchasing this book and for working with me to improve your life and set your goals. I look forward to working with you again within my next book or maybe at one of my seminars or workshops. Take care and may God bless you with all that you righteously desire.

A. Charles Strong

a_charles_strong@hotmail.com

Printed in the United Kingdom
by Lightning Source UK Ltd.
114731UKS00001B/99